Aboriginal Global Pioneers
Book 3

# Australian Aboriginal Religion

*Country and Dreaming*

Marji Hill

Published by The Prison Tree Press 2024
Copyright © 2024 Marji Hill

The Prison Tree Press
Suite 124
1-10 Albert Avenue
Broadbeach, Queensland 4218
https://marjihill.com
https://www.fastselfpublishing.com

Disclaimer:
All the material contained in this book is provided for educational and informational purposes only. No responsibility can be taken for any results or outcomes resulting from the use of this material.

While every care has been taken to trace and acknowledge copyright the publishers tender their apologies for any accidental infringement where copyright has proved untraceable.

Every attempt has been made to provide information that is both accurate and effective, however, the author does not assume any responsibility for the accuracy or use/misuse of this information."

A catalogue record for this work is available from the National Library of Australia

Acknowledgement is given to Canva for most of the illustrations in this book.

Aboriginal Global Pioneers (Series of 5 Books)
  Australian Aboriginal Origins: Earliest Beginnings (Book 1)
  Australian Aboriginal Trade: Sharing Goods and Services (Book 2)
  Australian Aboriginal Religion: Country and Dreaming (Book 3)
  Australian Aboriginal Fire: Managing Country (Book 4)
  Australian Aboriginal Medicine: Caring for People (Book 5)

ISBN  978-0-9756571-6-4  Hardback
ISBN  978-0-9756571-7-1  eBook

Australian Non-Fiction | First Nations | History

# Acknowledgements

I acknowledge the Traditional Custodians of Country
throughout Australia
and their connections to land, sea, and community.

I pay my respect to elders, past, present, and emerging
and extend my respect to all First Nations peoples today.

In the spirit of reconciliation,
my mission is to increase understanding
between the First Nations and other Australians
and to provide people from all over the globe
some basic understanding of Australia's first people,
their history, and cultures.

*Marji Hill*

# Contents

# INTRODUCTION

First Nations people developed a religious, social and cultural life that recognised the essential link between mankind and the land.

Burial rituals that happened 40,000 years ago demonstrated that First Nations people had religious beliefs. The human skeletons found at Lake Mungo in southwestern New South Wales were stained with red ochre.

This archaeological evidence indicates that Australia's First Nations people practised religious rituals all those years ago and had a firmly held belief in the afterlife.

As part of the world's oldest continuing civilisation, First Nations people were global pioneers in religion.

# DREAMTIME

The religious beliefs of First Nations people are commonly known as the Dreamtime — that time when all life and culture were created.

Ancestral beings emerged from a dark, dead, and silent world. These Dreamtime heroes moved over a featureless earth.

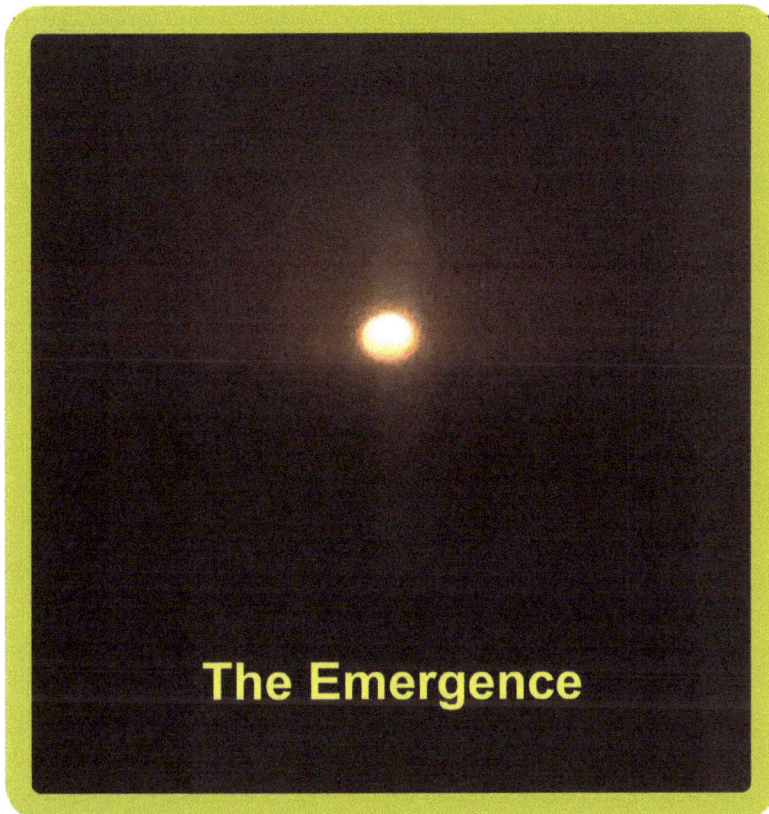

**The Emergence**

They journeyed across the continent moving across country. The places where they first appeared and the land that they covered on their journeys became the billabongs, the rivers, the rocks, the hills and mountains and all the features of the universe.

**They left behind the rocks and the trees**

They left behind the caverns, the rocks, the shady pools with their own spirit children. They left all living things — people, plants, animals, insects, fish and birds.

**They left behind all living things**

The great Ancestral beings had many adventures as they journeyed across the continent. Everything in the universe was created — the country, its geographical features and all living things.

**Everything in the universe was created**

When the deeds of creation were completed, the Ancestral beings retreated into Country. They went into places from where they could watch over the land and its people.

These were special locations and they could also be dangerous places.

When ceremonies were performed the creative powers of the Ancestral beings would again flow, renewing and reinvigorating the spirit force that flowed through the land and through all beings that lived in it.

The spirit force gave new life. It strengthened the spiritual bonds which bound people in unity to one another and to particular animals, plants and places with which they shared a common spirit.

# TOTEMS

The link between humans and all living things in nature and the Dreamtime are totems.

First Nations people are bound to the land by these spiritual links.

The kangaroo is a manifestation of the Giant Kangaroo Ancestor.

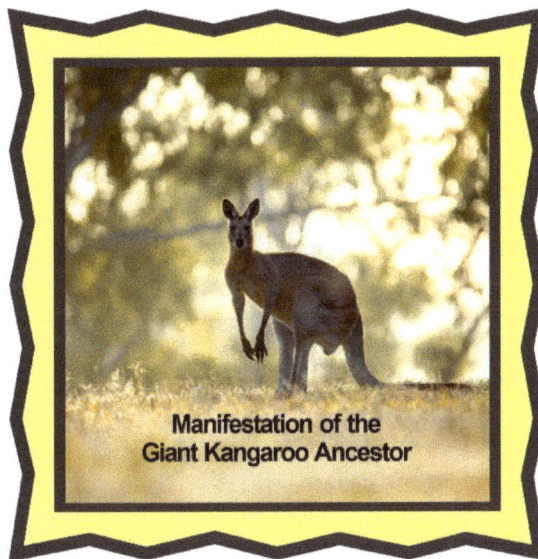

**Manifestation of the Giant Kangaroo Ancestor**

The emu is the Emu Ancestor.

Ancestral beings established the boundaries, the sacred sites and the religious ceremonies that connected people to Country and its conservation. They created an interconnected system of relationships and a set of rules for all to live by. While their presence was hidden they remained a vital force.

The Ancestral beings can intervene in the lives of the people they had created. Ceremonies are performed to harness their power.

Humans get their spiritual identification from totems at birth or just before they were born. It is called their Dreaming. If a person has a special link to the magpie, the magpie becomes that person's totem.

One or other parent might observe an unusual phenomenon.

A goanna might suddenly stand upright to block the parent's path, a species of fish could leap from the water near the parent, or a screeching parrot might, all of a sudden, fly from a nearby bush. A magpie may have flown into the path of the mother as she was out walking.

**A magpie may have flown into the path of the mother as she was out walking.**

This tells the parent the totemic group that the child belongs to. This becomes the child's personal totem.

The child, for example, will be linked to the Magpie totem or to the Goanna or to the Parrot or Fish.

When asked about their totem, a First Nations person might say, "I'm a Magpie", or a Wallaby, a Barramundi or an Echidna.

Totems link a person to the Dreamtime, to all living things, and to the land itself. People who share the same totem also have a special link to each other.

Throughout the bearer's life, that totem defines a whole area of relationship and responsibility to the totemic group who share that totem.

Children inherit their family ancestry from their parents. They are given rights and responsibilities in both their father's and their mother's family country.

They are given their social position in relation to those who are not members of their immediate family.

# RITUAL LEARNING

Among other things this tells people who, among these other families, are potential marriage partners.

The importance of the parents establishing the child's spirit source, a personal totem, is that it determines the child's essential being from the very beginning of his or her life.

It tells where the child's spirit has come from, and where it will return to when it departs the body. It establishes the spiritual responsibilities the child will share throughout all phases of life with those who share that totem.

Most importantly it maps the path the child will follow while growing to spiritual and social maturity.

That path will progress through a series of spiritual initiations. These begin at puberty and continue as long as they accept the responsibilities that go with the knowledge they acquire.

These learnings continue until their middle and later years when they have become adept at all the laws that is theirs to learn.

Who and what they are is revealed to them step by step in these initiations — the social and spiritual self which was theirs from the moment of their spiritual conception is unveiled. They learn progressively, as does the community to which they belong.

Each initiation moves them to a higher level of spiritual and social responsibility. From being minor performers in ceremonial ritual, they become ritual leaders and managers.

They become the senior people or elders, charged with watching over the law for their group. The elders are the decision makers. They are the judges, the peace keepers, the negotiators, and guardians of the group's traditions and knowledge.

They are the teachers who see that the young men and women, over time, come to know who and what they are.

Seniority is the privilege of those who respect the law and accept the responsibilities each new revelation brings.

Being yourself then, in the First Nations tradition, means achieving the fullness of the identity each person possesses from the moment of his/her spiritual conception.

# ORAL TRADITIONS

The oral traditions of First Nations people are central to their cultures and remain alive today. Much is being done to record these traditions and to convert the stories into written form.

The oral traditions tell the sagas of the Dreamtime of many thousands of years ago. They are more than just tales; they hold the beliefs, values, and histories of First Nations societies.

Passed down through generations by storytelling, these stories explain how various geographical features like mountains, rivers, and valleys came to be. They also tell us about the creation of plants, animals and even human beings.

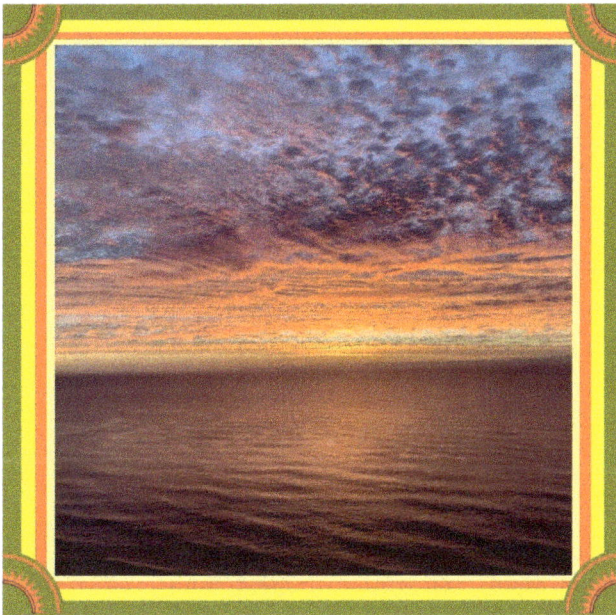

**Creation**

Imagine a place where every star, hill, river, and tree holds a story and a meaning that has been passed down through countless generations.

These oral traditions convey details about the land and its significance.

For instance, a story might describe how a giant snake created a winding river as it slithered across the earth.

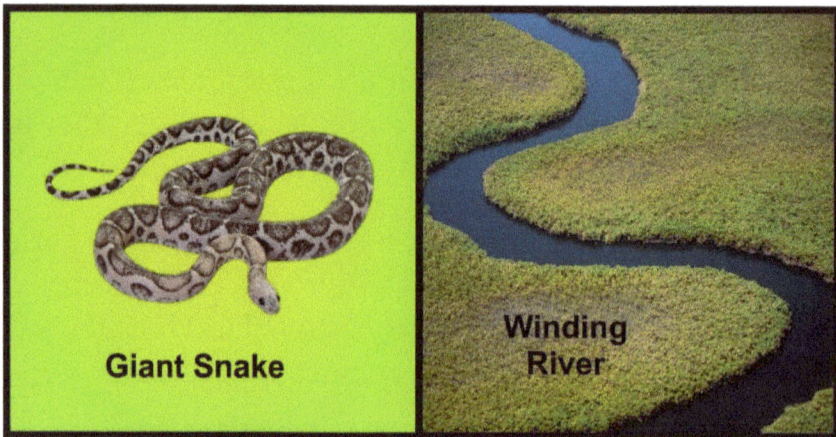

**Giant Snake**　　**Winding River**

Such stories imbue the land with spiritual meaning, identity for those with that totem and serve as a guide for living harmoniously with nature.

This connection to the land is reinforced every time these stories are told. This ensures that the knowledge is passed down from the senior people to children and from one generation to the next.

In addition to the stories, ceremonies play an equally crucial role in keeping Dreamtime alive.

In these ceremonies, Dreamtime sagas are brought to life through song, dance, carvings, and paintings.

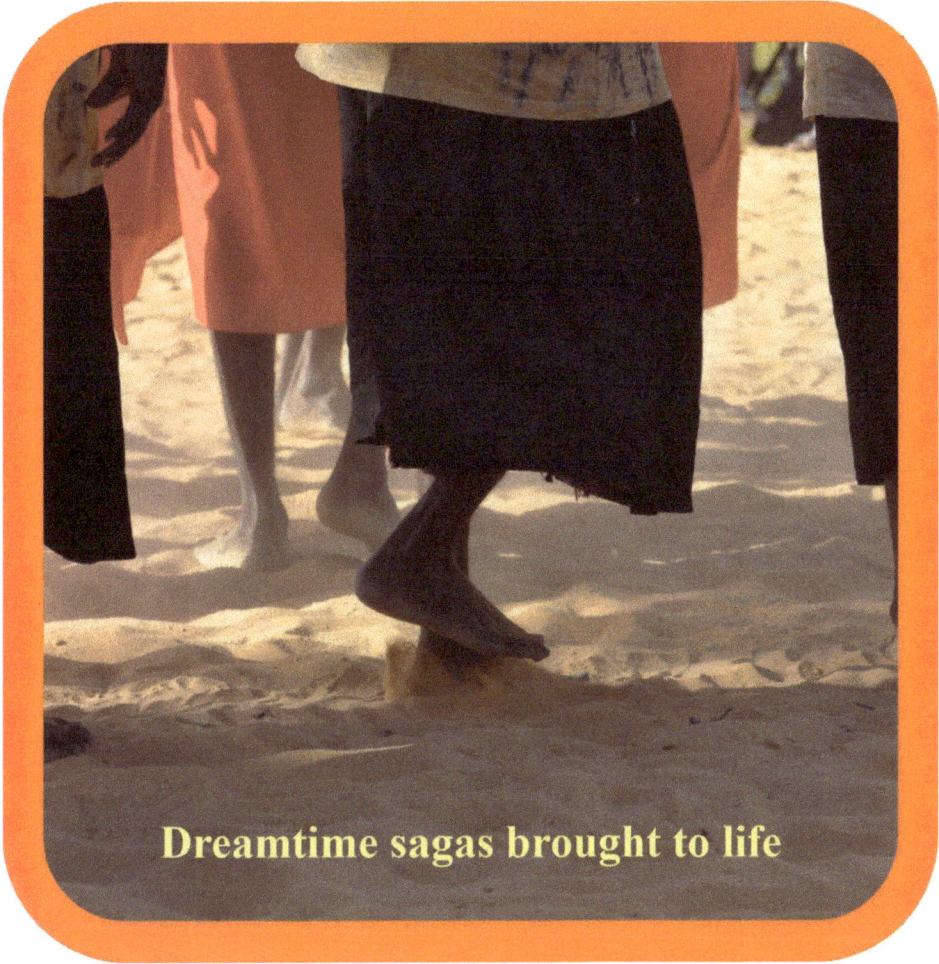

Dreamtime sagas brought to life

These artistic expressions evoke the power of Ancestral beings, making the past vividly present. For example, a dance might mimic the movements of an animal spirit, while a painting might depict a significant Dreamtime event.

Oral traditions play a vital role in preserving the rich heritage of the Dreamtime among Australia's First Nations peoples.

Dreamtime is not just about creation stories; it is a deeply spiritual connection that forms the foundation of First Nations cultures. It explains how everything came into being through the actions of the powerful Ancestral beings.

For example, the Ancestral spirit being, Kaaloo, the tiny pure white rat set the waters free to flow in the land of the Gulngai people in North Queensland.

A story about Emu and Brolga from the Nunggubuyu people in Arnhem Land in the Northern Territory tells how Emu is lazy and greedy while Brolga goes to work collecting food.

There are many stories about the rainbow serpent.

One is about a rainbow snake called Ambidj which swallowed a lot of people from Goulburn Island. After this Ambidj was chased up a creek and speared to death. The hunters cut open the snake to rescue the people it swallowed. At the place where Ambidj died there is now a big freshwater lagoon which never gets dry.

Spirit beings other than the great ancestral heroes inhabit the countryside. Some shy spirits live in the dark crevices of rocks and caves or dwell in waterholes. Some spirits are mischievous and others are powerful and can intervene in the lives of people.

**A site of special significance**

The Ancestral beings travelled across the countryside in the Dreamtime shaping it, planting and peopling the land. Their journeys crisscrossed the Australian continent. Along these ancestral tracks are sites of special significance where certain events and incidents happened.

Think about a mountain towering high above. To many, it's just a natural structure, but to First Nations people, it holds the spirits of these Ancestral beings. Similarly, a serene pool of water or an intricately shaped rock can be a site of spiritual significance.

Ancestral beings didn't just create animals and plants arbitrarily. Each species carries the spirit of these beings, making every creature sacred.

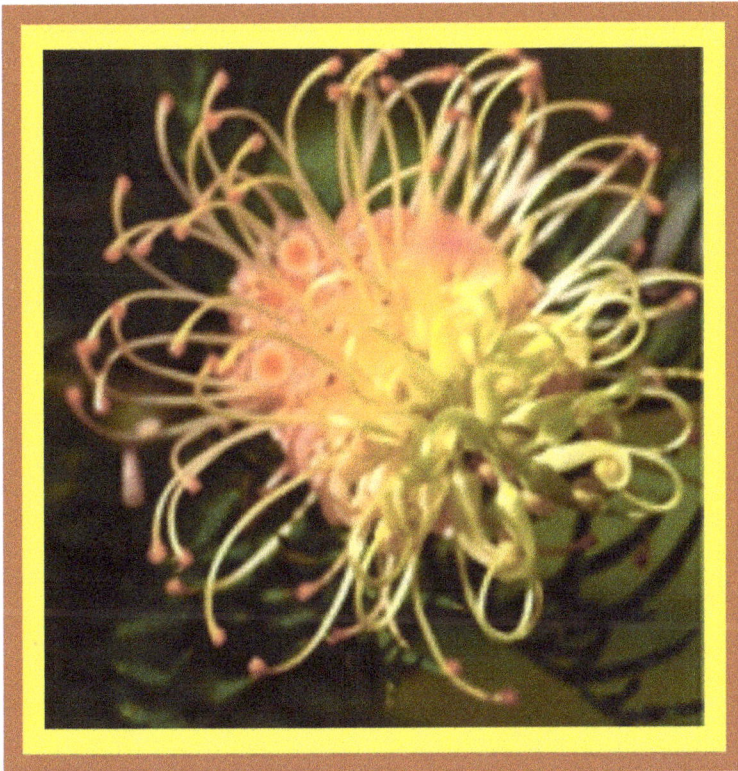

**Species carry the spirit of beings**

Whether it is a kangaroo hopping through the bush or a eucalyptus tree swaying in the wind, both are seen as embodiments of the ancestral spirits. This belief imbues nature with a sense of reverence, teaching respect for all forms of life.

These places in the land serve as reminders both of the Ancestral beings' presence as well as their creative deeds.

These special places might therefore be dangerous to people who do not permitted there. Even people who do belong must take care to warn the spirit of the place that they are coming to visit. These places are the most revered places in First Nations religion. They are very secret; they are sacred.

Ancestral beings remain active, even though you cannot see them. Their anger is to be feared and avoided at all times.

# CEREMONIES

A major story or song cycle is part of ceremonial ritual. A ceremony evokes the power of Ancestral beings and encourages them to release again their creative powers.

Great creative sagas are re-enacted in song and dance. Days can be spent in preparation for a ceremony making carvings, paintings, sand sculptures and other ritual items.

There are different kinds of ceremonies.

Public ceremonies are for the enjoyment of men, women and children in which they take part. These are mainly to do with every day activities such as hunting and food gathering.

Some religious ceremonies are public in which everyone can participate. Others are partially secret from which women and children are excluded.

Then there are the secret, sacred ceremonies. These are only for initiated men or women. Men have their secret ceremonies and women have theirs. Secret male ceremonies are restricted to men initiated into that particular grouping and to those about to be initiated into the ceremony.

Women have their own secret ceremonies from which men are excluded.

# BORA GROUNDS

Bora grounds are sacred ceremonial spaces where many important rituals take place.

One of the most significant ceremonies held at Bora grounds is the initiation ceremony. These rites mark the transition from childhood to adulthood and impart essential knowledge about laws, responsibilities, and cultural practices.

Initiation ceremonies are particularly important because they educate young people about their roles within the community. During these ceremonies, senior people teach initiates the laws and customs they must follow.

**Educating young people**

Many of the ceremonial grounds found in eastern Australia were attached by a path to a preparation ground. When the preparations for the ceremonies were completed the participants moved from the preparation area to the ceremonial ground.

These are called "bora" grounds. They might dance their way there singing verses of the song cycle which belong to that particular ceremony.

First Nations religious ceremonies are a whole complex of dance, song, body decoration, sculpture, paintings and other ritual objects. There are sounds of musical accompaniment, cries, and shouts from the participants, clapping and stamping, flaring torches, sounds and smells.

Those taking part in the ceremony dress up and paint themselves to represent the Ancestral beings.

Some ceremonies are associated with "rites of passage", marking important stages in a person's life. The first initiation marks the beginning of adulthood.

This is important because it sets the child on the path to adult knowledge of law and religion. This sort of knowledge cannot be given to the uninitiated.

# INITIATION CEREMONIES

Ceremonies for male initiation are more elaborate than for women.

Initiation ceremonies for boys occurs around the ages of ten and sixteen years. They must show that they are prepared to respect the law that will be revealed to them.

All of the law will not be revealed to them at their first initiation. Greater revelations will come over time so long as they show themselves to be worthy guardians of the law and its mysteries.

Details of initiation ceremonies will vary from group to group. The main purpose of the ceremony is to mark the changes from childhood to adulthood and to emphasise the importance of this change in a person's life.

While a boy will know that he is soon to be initiated, he will not know when exactly. The senior men know when and where the ceremony will take place.

When the time comes the boys are isolated from the other children and women. The boys are painted and men around them chant the verses of the initiation songs. There is clapping of clap sticks and the stamping of feet as the boys are taken into the ceremonial ground.

# FUNERAL CEREMONIES

When a person dies customs for handling grief vary throughout First Nations cultures. The customs always include marked displays of sorrow and distress.

Funeral ceremonies and disposal of the body are also complex and varied, the main purpose being to ensure the safe return of the spirit to its totemic spirit home.

There were different ways of disposing of the dead. This could include burial in the ground or in a tree, a cave or rock shelter, or the body could be placed on a free standing platform.

Funeral ceremonies are usually long and complex and could continue on long after the disposal of the corpse.

In many communities there is the custom of refraining from using the name of the deceased and to cover over any image of the dead person.

The diversity of ceremonies reflects the complexity and richness of First Nations cultures. Each type of ceremony, whether public, partially secret, or fully secret, has a unique set of rules and participants.

# OWNERSHIP OF LAND

First Nations people own land in a spiritual sense and this ownership is connected to religion. The events of the Dreamtime tell which group of people own which areas of land.

With ownership of land comes ritual responsibilities. Ritual owners have to ensure that ceremonies or rituals are performed at the proper times and proper place and that the ceremony is performed correctly. Because many people are brought together for a ceremony, a lot of organisation has to be done.

Ceremonial preparations can take days. The dance ground has to be prepared, ritual paraphernalia made, bodies have to be painted. And because so many people are involved it is always important to hold ceremonies when there is plenty of food available in the bush.

Ownership of land is inherited from the father. It is also possible to inherit certain responsibilities for the mother's family land and ceremonies. While a First Nations person can be an owner of the land, he or she can also be a manager of the land and its ceremonies.

In the religious aspect, the roles of owners and managers have to make sure that the spirit forces in the land are respected. These spirit forces must continue to use their powers for the good of all living things.

The owners and managers have to make sure that the rituals are practised properly and that the laws laid down in the Dreamtime are obeyed.

The rich tapestry of Dreamtime stories and cultural practices continues to thrive. Oral traditions and ceremonies remain integral to the identity and cohesion of Australia's First Nations peoples.

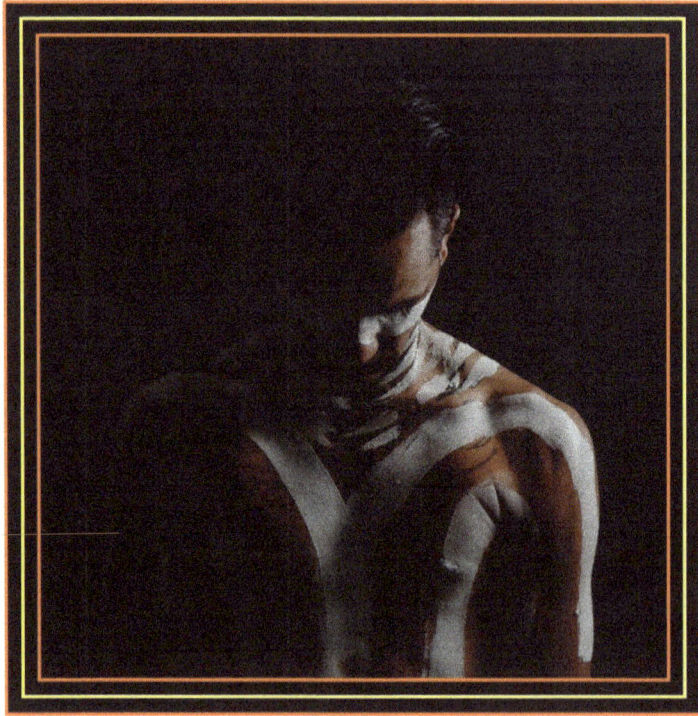

**Honouring ancestors**

They provide a vital link between the past, present, and future. By preserving and celebrating these traditions, the communities honour their ancestors and ensure that their wisdom endures for generations to come.

# Glossary

**Embodiments**  A tangible or visible form of an idea, quality, or feeling

**Manifestation** When something is made real

**Revelations**  A surprising and previously unknown fact that has been disclosed to others

**Reverence**  Deep respect for someone or something

**Rites of passage**  A ceremony or event marking an important stage in someone's life, especially birth, the transition from childhood to adulthood, marriage, and death

# Sources

The author acknowledges the following sources:

Barlow, Alex 1994 *Australian Aboriginal Religions*. South Melbourne, Vic, Macmillan

Barlow, Alex & Hill, Marji 1987 *The Land and the Dreaming: Aboriginal Religions.* South Melbourne, Vic, Macmillan

Hill, Marji 2021 *First People Then and Now: Introducing Indigenous Australians*. 2nd ed. Broadbeach, Qld, The Prison Tree Press

# Who is Marji Hill

Marji Hill, artist and painter since childhood, runs her art career alongside her career as an author.

She is a highly respected international author as well as a seasoned business executive, researcher and coach.

Marji is passionate about promoting understanding between Australia's first people and other Australians.

The spirit of reconciliation was fostered in all her writings ever since she was a Research Fellow in Education at the Australian Institute of Aboriginal and Torres Strait Islander Studies (AIATSIS) in Canberra.

From 2008 to 2011, Marji was Deputy Chairperson of the Mosman Branch of Reconciliation Australia in Sydney.

Following her Research Fellowship at AIATSIS in 1976 Marji, together with her late partner, Alex Barlow, produced more than seventy (70) books on all aspects of the First Nations people including the critical, annotated bibliography *Black Australia*.

In 1989 she was the Project Coordinator and one of the researchers and writers of *Australian Aboriginal Culture* the official Australian Government publication on First Nations people.

In 1988 *Six Australian Battlefields* was published by Angus and Robertson. A decade later it was re-published by Allen & Unwin as a paperback edition.

Her nine-volume encyclopaedia, *Macmillan Encyclopaedia of Australia's Aboriginal Peoples* was published in 2000 and in 2009 she published *The Apology: Saying Sorry To The Stolen Generations.*

Marji's more recent publications extend to self-improvement and self-help with books like *Staying Young Growing Old* and *Inspired by Country* a self-help book about painting with gouache.

# More Books by Marji Hill

## First Nations

Hill, Marji 2021 *Australian Aboriginal History: 5 Stories of Indigenous Heroes.* Broadbeach, Qld, The Prison Tree Press.

Hill, Marji 2021 *First People Then and Now: Introducing Indigenous Australians.* 2nd ed. Broadbeach, Qld, The Prison Tree Press.

## Aboriginal Global Pioneers

Hill, Marji 2024 *Australian Aboriginal Origins: Earliest Beginnings.* Broadbeach, Qld, The Prison Tree Press. (Book 1)

Hill, Marji 2024 *Australian Aboriginal Trade: Sharing Goods and Services.* Broadbeach, Qld, The Prison Tree Press. (Book 2)

Hill, Marji 2024 *Australian Aboriginal Religion: Country and Dreaming.* Broadbeach, Qld, The Prison Tree Press. (Book 3)

Hill, Marji 2024 *Australian Aboriginal Fire: Managing Country.* Broadbeach, Qld, The Prison Tree Press. (Book 4)

Hill, Marji 2024 *Australian Aboriginal Medicine: Caring for People.* Broadbeach, Qld, The Prison Tree Press. (Book 5)

## Self-improvement/Self-Help

Hill, Marji 2014 *Staying Young Growing Old.* Broadbeach, Qld, The Prison Tree Press.

Hill, Marji 2020 *How Big Is Your Why? An Author's Guide to Time Management and Productivity to Achieve Transformational Results.* Broadbeach, Qld, The Prison Tree Press.

Hill, Marji 2020 *A Create and Publish Toolbox: 101 Prompts In A Guided Journal To Help You Write, Self-publish, And Market Your Book On Amazon.* Broadbeach, Qld, The Prison Tree Press.

Hill, Marji 2021 *Inspired by Country: An Artist's Journey Back to Nature, Landscape Painting with Gouache.* Broadbeach, Qld, The Prison Tree Press.

Hill, Marji 2024 *Australian Paintings: Artworks by Marji Hill.* Broadbeach, Qld, The Prison Tree Press.

## Gold

Hill, Marji 2022 *Gates of Gold: The Discovery of Gold, its Legacy and its Contribution to Australian Identity* Broadbeach, Qld, The Prison Tree Press.

Hill, Marji 2022 *Shadows of Gold: Eureka and the Birth of Australian Democracy.* Broadbeach, Qld, The Prison Tree Press.

Hill, Marji 2022 *Gold and the Chinese: Racism, Riots and Protest on the Australian Goldfields.* Broadbeach, Qld, The Prison Tree Press.

Hill, Marji 2022 *Ghosts of Gold: The Life and Times of Jupiter Mosman.* Broadbeach, Qld, The Prison Tree Press.

Hill, Marji 2022 *Blood Gold: Native Police, Bushrangers & Law and Order on the Goldfields.* Broadbeach, Qld, The Prison Tree Press.

www.ingramcontent.com/pod-product-compliance
Lightning Source LLC
Chambersburg PA
CBHW040835300326
41914CB00060B/1356